TRADITIONS AND CELEBRATIONS

VALENTINE'S DAY

by Steve Foxe

PEBBLE
a capstone imprint

Published by Pebble, an imprint of Capstone
1710 Roe Crest Drive, North Mankato, Minnesota 56003
capstonepub.com

Copyright © 2024 by Capstone. All rights reserved. No part of this publication may be reproduced in whole or in part, or stored in a retrieval system, or transmitted in any form or by any means, electronic, mechanical, photocopying, recording, or otherwise, without written permission of the publisher.

Library of Congress Cataloging-in-Publication Data is available on the Library of Congress website.

ISBN: 9780756576943 (hardcover)
ISBN: 9780756577247 (paperback)
ISBN: 9780756577254 (ebook PDF)

Summary: Valentine's Day is about celebrating love. Around the world, people show their affection for others on this special day. Some people exchange cards or paper hearts. Others give chocolate pigs or other candy. Discover how people around the world celebrate Valentine's Day.

Editorial Credits
Editor: Ericka Smith; Designer: Kayla Rossow; Media Researcher: Svetlana Zhurkin; Production Specialist: Katy LaVigne

Image Credits
Getty Images: AFP/Jung Yeon-Je, 27, Archive Photos/Kean Collection, 23, Jose Luis Pelaez Inc., 20, manonallard, 29, Milko, 22, NurPhoto/George Calvelo, 28, Peter Dazeley, 11, SeventyFour, 19, Wiphop Sathawirawong, 18; Newscom: Heritage Images AiWire/Heritage Art/Sir James Thornhill, 17; Shutterstock: beeboys, 5, C. Nass, 24, Creative Family, 25, Katya Rekina, 4, Rafal Kulik (background), back cover and throughout, Stefania Valvola, 8, 15, Svetlana Kolpakova, 21, VictoriaArt, cover, yurakrasil, 1; Superstock: Universal Images/PHAS, 7, Universal Images/Pictures from History, 13

All internet sites appearing in back matter were available and accurate when this book was sent to press.

Printed and bound in China. 5593

TABLE OF CONTENTS

WHAT IS VALENTINE'S DAY? 4

WHEN IS VALENTINE'S DAY? 14

WHO CELEBRATES
VALENTINE'S DAY? 18

HOW DO PEOPLE CELEBRATE
VALENTINE'S DAY? 20

GLOSSARY...30

READ MORE....................................... 31

INTERNET SITES 31

INDEX.. 32

ABOUT THE AUTHOR 32

Words in **bold** are in the glossary.

WHAT IS VALENTINE'S DAY?

Heart-shaped decorations hang in store windows. Couples give each other chocolates. People write love notes to their crushes. Valentine's Day is a day to celebrate love!

Valentine's Day takes its name from a Christian saint. But no one's sure exactly which one. Originally, it was a day of feasting. Over time, the day became a day about love. Now, it's for couples, crushes, and candy.

THE LEGEND OF SAINT VALENTINE

There are at least three stories about Saint Valentine. The most common one takes place in Rome, Italy. It happened during the third century. It's about a Christian priest named Father Valentinus.

At the time, Christians were punished or killed for spreading their beliefs. Father Valentinus was arrested for preaching about Christianity.

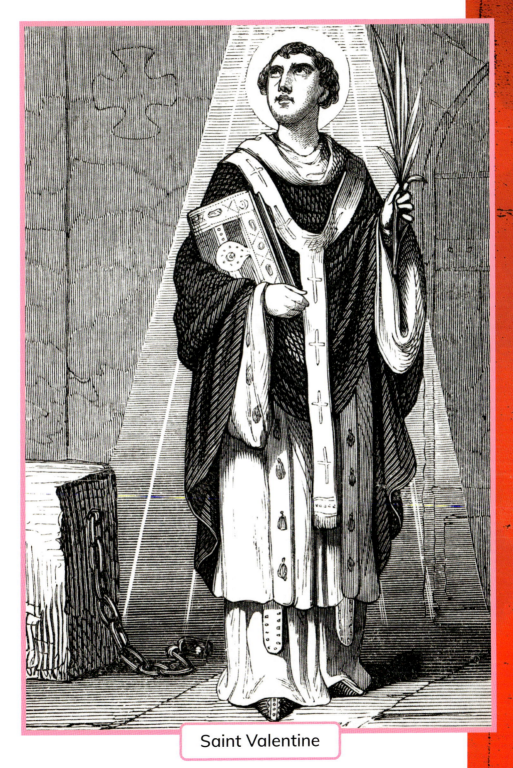

Saint Valentine

Saint Valentine

In the story, a man named Asterius was in charge of punishing Father Valentinus. Father Valentinus tried to **convert** Asterius to Christianity. Asterius agreed that he would convert if Valentinus could prove Christianity was real.

Asterius had a blind daughter. He asked Father Valentinus to make her see again. Father Valentinus placed his hands on her eyes. He prayed. Afterward, the girl could see again.

Asterius's whole family converted. When the Roman emperor learned about this, he had Father Valentinus and Asterius's family killed.

In some versions of the story, Father Valentinus and Asterius's daughter fell in love. While Valentinus waited to be killed, he wrote her a note. He signed it, "Your Valentine." This may have inspired the tradition of sending love letters.

Valentine's Day didn't involve romance until the 14th century. The writer Geoffrey Chaucer published the poem *Parliament of Fowls*. The poem contained these lines: "For this was on Saint Valentine's Day / When every bird comes there to choose his match."

Chaucer was referring to birds nesting together on Valentine's Day. After he published the poem, people began to associate the day with couples falling in love.

Geoffrey Chaucer

WHEN IS VALENTINE'S DAY?

Valentine's Day takes place on February 14 in most places. This is the day that some believe Saint Valentine died.

In some Christian faiths, the day a saint dies is observed each year. Usually, there is a feast on that day. When Valentine's Day was first celebrated in the eighth century, it was an **annual** feast.

A Valentine's Day celebration in Italy

Some historians believe Valentine's Day replaced an ancient Roman festival called Lupercalia. It took place in February. Between February 13 and 15, Romans held large parties. Men and women paired up to celebrate. After the festival, many of them married.

Lupercalia was a **pagan** tradition. Some pagan traditions were later replaced with Christian ones. Valentine's Day takes place around the same time as Lupercalia, so the Christian holiday might have replaced the pagan festival.

Lupercalia

WHO CELEBRATES VALENTINE'S DAY?

Although Valentine's Day has a Christian beginning, all sorts of people celebrate it now. Most often, Valentine's Day is a day for couples. People who are dating might give each other gifts. Married couples might celebrate by going out to dinner.

But Valentine's Day can also be a day to celebrate all kinds of love. Families and friends **exchange** Valentine's Day cards and gifts too.

HOW DO PEOPLE CELEBRATE VALENTINE'S DAY?

People celebrate Valentine's Day in many different ways. Hearts are a popular symbol for love and affection. Chocolates and flowers are common gifts in many cultures too.

UNITED STATES

Valentine's Day is extremely popular in the United States. Every year, Americans spend billions of dollars on cards, candy, and gifts. Small candy hearts with messages on them are often given as gifts.

Cupid is a beloved symbol of Valentine's Day in the United States and Europe. Cupid is a figure from Greek and Roman **mythology**. He is usually depicted as a small child with wings. He shoots arrows. It is said that anyone struck by Cupid's arrows will fall in love.

GERMANY

In Germany, Valentine's Day is only for adults. One popular German tradition is to exchange chocolate pigs. The pigs represent luck and love. German couples also share heart-shaped gingerbread cookies with messages written on them.

Snowdrops

DENMARK

In Denmark, friends, family, and couples exchange cards that have sweet or silly messages. The silly cards are often signed with dots. The woman who receives one must guess the name of the man who sent it. These cards often contain pressed white flowers called snowdrops.

SOUTH AFRICA

In South Africa, there's less guessing on Valentine's Day. Women write the names of their crushes on heart-shaped paper. Then they pin that paper to their sleeves.

SOUTH KOREA

In South Korea, women buy gifts and chocolate for their male partners. Men do the same thing a month later on White Day. There is also a Black Day later in the year for single people.

PHILIPPINES

Across the Philippines, Valentine's Day is all about marriage. Mass weddings are held around the country. The government **sponsors** many of them. The large weddings started as a way for people without much money to have nice weddings.

A mass wedding in the Philippines

Whether you celebrate Valentine's Day with a romantic partner, a friend, or a family member, it is a day of love. Exchanging gifts or spending time together is a way to show someone that you care about them. You can show your love any day of the year, but Valentine's Day is extra special!

GLOSSARY

annual (AN-yoo-uhl)—happening once every year

convert (kuhn-VURT)—to change from one religion or faith to another

exchange (iks-CHAYNJ)—to give something and receive something in return

mythology (mi-THOL-uh-jee)—old or ancient stories told again and again that help connect people with their past

pagan (PAY-gun)—related to belief systems other than Judaism, Islam, or Christianity

sponsor (SPON-sur)—to pay for an event or project

READ MORE

Anderson, Shannon. *Celebrating Valentine's Day: History, Traditions, and Activities—A Holiday Book for Kids*. Emeryville, CA: Rockridge Press, 2021.

Foxe, Steve. *Pride Month*. North Mankato, MN: Capstone, 2024.

Mansfield, Nicole A. *Easter*. North Mankato, MN: Capstone, 2024.

INTERNET SITES

Britannica Kids: Valentine's Day
kids.britannica.com/kids/article/Valentines-Day/390980

Kiddle: Valentine's Day Facts for Kids
kids.kiddle.co/Valentine%27s_Day

National Geographic Kids: Valentine's Day
kids.nationalgeographic.com/celebrations/article/valentines-day

INDEX

Asterius, 9–10

Black Day, 26

Chaucer, Geoffrey, 12–13

Cupid, 23

Denmark, 25

Father Valentinus, 6–11. *See also* Saint Valentine.

Germany, 24

Italy, 6, 15

Lupercalia, 16–17

Philippines, 28

Rome, Italy, 6

Saint Valentine, 5, 6–11, 12

South Africa, 26

South Korea, 26

United States, 22–23

White Day, 26

ABOUT THE AUTHOR

Steve Foxe is the Eisner and Ringo Award-nominated author of more than 75 comics and children's books including *X-Men '92: House of XCII*, *Rainbow Bridge*, *Adventure Kingdom*, and the *Spider-Ham* series from Scholastic. He has written for properties like Spider-Man, Pokémon, Mario, LEGO City, Batman, Justice League, Baby Shark, and many more. He celebrates his valentines—his partner and their dog—every day of the year.